Erosion on Earth

CONCEPT SCIENCE

Written by Colin Walker • Illustrated by Linda McClelland

Most things change as they get older.
Plants and animals change
as they get older.
We change as we get older too.

The earth also changes.
It erodes or wears away.

When big waves and storms crash against the land, parts of the land are worn away. This is called erosion.

Rivers cause erosion.
When a river floods,
soil, rocks and stones get swept away.
They are sometimes swept out to sea.

If rain falls on bare ground,
the earth can be eroded or worn away.

Dust storms can cause erosion.
Sharp dust can wear away the surface
of very hard rocks.

Rocks worn away by the wind
may form very strange shapes.

Big sand dunes can be moved to different places by the wind.

Glaciers of ice and rock
grind against the earth,
and wear it away.

Earthquakes may change the surface of the earth.
Earthquakes can cause erosion.

Volcanoes emit hot rocks and lava.
The lava may cover forests
that protect the land from erosion.

Erosion is wearing away our earth's surface.
Erosion may happen quickly or slowly,
but it is happening all the time.

QUIZ

Ask your friend these questions. . .

The wearing away of the earth's surface is called ____________.

How do  cause erosion?

 are worn away by the wind.

How are 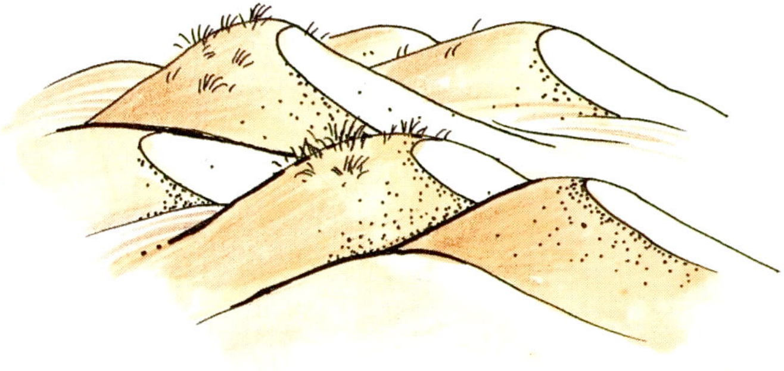 moved to different places?

Can earthquakes cause erosion?

Can a  cause erosion?

Some things to do by yourself or as a group

1. Build a sand castle. Sketch the shape of it. Fill a watering can and gently pour water over the sand castle. Sketch the shape of the sand castle after you have poured half of the water from the can, and again after you have poured all the water from the can. Compare the pictures.